LANGUAGE ARTS 606
Poetry

LANGUAGE
ARTS

LIFEPAC Test is located in the center of the booklet. Please remove before starting the unit.

Author:
Annis Shepherd

Editor-in-Chief:
Richard W. Wheeler, M.A.Ed.

Editor:
Elizabeth Loeks Bouman

Consulting Editor:
Rudolph Moore, Ph.D.

Revision Editor:
Alan Christopherson, M.S.

MEDIA CREDITS:
Page 7: © Hoatzinexp iStock, Thinkstock; **8:** © Eremin Sergey, Dreamstime; **28:** Shaiith, iStock,Thinkstock; **38:** © Andrejs Pidjass iStock, Thinkstock; **42:** © cate_89 iStock, Thinkstock; © Alexander Kukushkin, Dreamstime; © Madartists, Dreamstime, © Hrigoriy Donskoi, Dreamstime; **51:** © Bobby Deal, Dreamstime.

Alpha Omega
PUBLICATIONS

804 N. 2nd Ave. E.
Rock Rapids, IA 51246-1759

Poetry

Introduction

This LIFEPAC® includes various poetic forms such as free verse, pen pictures, Ezra Pound couplets, limericks, ballads, lullabies, and mood poems. It also will cover similes, metaphors, alliteration, palindromes, riddles, and other word puzzles. All these poetic forms and techniques help color our language and make it more fascinating to read and listen to.

As you progress through the LIFEPAC, notice how the different poetic forms use rhythm, rhyme, and spacing. Noticing these forms will help you when you start writing poems of your own. The exercises and puzzles will help you test your power with words and your writing skills.

Objectives

Read these objectives. The objectives tell you what you should be able to do when you have successfully completed this LIFEPAC. Each section will list according to the numbers below what objectives will be met in that section. When you have finished this LIFEPAC, you should be able to:

1. Identify certain poetic styles.

2. Write poems of your own, using some of the poetic forms studied in this LIFEPAC.

3. List some of the major characteristics of poetry.

4. Identify effective rhyme and word choice.

5. Demonstrate economy of words in writing poetry.

6. Identify alliteration, similes, and metaphors.

7. Write palindromes and acronyms.

8. Select and apply word inflections.

9. Spell and use some new homonyms.

10. Identify patterns in words.

11. Write the definitions of some vocabulary words.

12. Identify sounds and their various spellings.

13. Use a basic vocabulary of literary terms.

14. Make an attractive book of your own poetry.

Survey the LIFEPAC. Ask yourself some questions about this study and write your questions here.

_____
_____
_____
_____
_____
_____
_____
_____
_____
_____
_____
_____
_____
_____
_____
_____
_____
_____
_____
_____
_____

1. SECTION ONE

This section will introduce to you the wonderful world of words. You will learn some of the major characteristics of poetry and the necessity of an expanded vocabulary. You will increase your understanding of free verse and narrative poems. You will also learn about word inflections and review the use of similes. You will learn to spell some general pattern words and some homonyms, and you will practice handwriting.

Section Objectives

Review these objectives. When you have completed this section, you should be able to:

3. List some of the major characteristics of poetry.
4. Identify effective rhyme and word choice.
6. Identify alliteration, similes, and metaphors.
8. Select and apply word inflections.
9. Spell and use some new homonyms.
10. Identify patterns in words.
11. Write the definitions of some vocabulary words.

Vocabulary

Study these words to enhance your learning success in this section.

chant (chant). To sing a short, simple song without melody.

constrain (kun strān'). To restrict something.

drowsily (drou' zu lē). In a sleepy way.

economy (i kon' u mē). Making the most of what one has; freedom from waste in the use of anything.

emphasis (em' fu sīs). Stress; special force of voice put on particular words or syllables.

epic (ep' ik). A long poem that tells of the adventures of one or more great heroes.

ford (fôrd). To cross a river, stream, or other body of water.

formal (fôr' mul). According to set customs or rules.

knots (nots). A measure of speed used on ships; one nautical mile per hour.

legendary (lej' un der' ē). Fabulous; like a legend.

monotonous (mu not' u nus). Not varying; without change; boring because it is always the same.

pliant (plī' unt). Bending easily; yielding.

repetition (rep' u tish' un). Doing again; saying again.

sated (sā' tud). Satisfied; complete; full.

Note: *All vocabulary words in this LIFEPAC appear in* **boldface** *print the first time they are used. If you are unsure of the meaning when you are reading, study the definitions given.*

Pronunciation Key: hat, āge, cãre, fär; let, ēqual, tėrm; it, īce; hot, ōpen, ôrder; oil; out; cup, pu̇t, rüle; child; long; thin; /ŦH/ for then; /zh/ for measure; /u/ or /ə/ represents /a/ in about, /e/ in taken, /i/ in pencil, /o/ in lemon, and /u/ in circus.

POETIC CHARACTERISTICS

Poetry is not a new word or form to you. When you listen to songs or records, when you hear commercials or jingles, when children **chant** rhymes as they jump rope, you are hearing poetry.

Rhythm. Whenever you hear rhythm, you are hearing a little poetry. Nature is full of rhythm. We talk, walk, and work in rhythm. For example, when you listen to a person, you may describe them as a monotonous or boring speaker or you may say they are entertaining or interesting to listen to. This difference is due to rhythm. A monotonous speaker uses poor rhythm. (Don't confuse rhythm with rhyme. We will talk about this difference later in the LIFEPAC.)

Rhythm is one characteristic of poetry. It is a natural, positive movement of sound, in this case, in words. You could describe rhythm as the beat stress or emotional **emphasis** of a word or a group of words.

Pattern. Another characteristic of poetry is pattern (**repetition** of something for effect). This characteristic can involve page pattern, line pattern, stanza pattern, word pattern, rhythm pattern, and sound pattern. Some of these patterns are explained in other sections of the LIFEPAC.

Central idea. Poetry usually has a central idea, expressed as simply and vividly as possible. In poetry, you need imagination. By being creative and thinking imaginatively, you make thoughts and words sound new and fresh.

Economy of words. Because poems are usually short when compared to a short story or a novel, the poet must be extra careful when choosing and placing words. Unnecessary words use up important space, so the poet throws them out. The poet wants to express as much as they can in the fewest words possible.

Economy of words, therefore, is another characteristic of poetry. Long poems that tell stories are called narrative poems. A ballad is a form of a narrative poem. An **epic** poem also tells a story, but usually it involves a **legendary** hero and tells about his heroic deeds. Even narrative poems, however, must be written with economy of words.

The following poem demonstrates many of the basic characteristics of poetry. The poem has rhythm, as you can tell by the beat. The poem has patterns–a four-line stanza pattern in which alternate lines rhyme. The poem has a central idea–the beautiful swift movement of a fish is like beautiful, swift thoughts of a person. The poem has economy of word–each phrase stands for a larger thought.

Fish

Pliant blades of silver light
Cut their way through **knots** of sea
They are thoughts of sheer delight
A fish–man, what joy to be!

- Annis Mather

Write what you think are the four main characteristics of poetry. Write these in the order they are given.

1.1 _____

1.2 _____

1.3 _____

1.4 _____

Write _E_ in front of the sentences that have good economy of words.

1.5 _____ It was a very special, wonderful day for Joe and the person who was with him, his best friend Marc.

1.6 _____ This little pig went to market.

1.7 _____ The wind is tearing the tree tops to shreds.

1.8 _____ What my friend said when she was speaking was just too full of humor to make it possible for me to believe her.

FREE VERSE

Free verse may be called poetic painting. The following two short poems are written in free verse. That is, they are not **constrained** by any **formal** pattern such as rhyme or a specific number of words or a certain number of lines. The poet is able to express their thoughts freely, which is why it is called "free verse."

See if you can pick out the rhythm of each. Does the rhythm repeat itself or is it different for each line? Does each poem deal with a central idea or topic? Do the poets select words whose sounds fit the mood of the poem? These characteristics will help you when you write your own poems. Learn to identify them.

Best of Two Worlds

Birds on a telephone wire

make the best of two worlds.

Sated with food from nature's feast

they rest after dinner.

And, unaware of the human talk

flowing silently beneath their feet,

They **drowsily** discuss where

they will dine tomorrow.

- Elizabeth Loeks Bouman

Read the poem "Best of Two Worlds," and explain how the birds enjoy the best of two worlds. Discuss the poem with a friend.

1.9 _____

_____

_____

_____

_____

_____

_____

FRIEND'S CHECK _____ _____

initials   date

Lost Youth

He thinks he's old at thirty. So he is!

No graying hair, nor stooping back,

As yet proclaim him so. But for him

There are no hills to climb, no streams to **ford**,

No depths to reach. He only sees his shadow

On the path. And no birds sing!

- Annis Mather

 Complete the following activities.

1.10 Write a short paragraph explaining what you think the poet means in "Lost Youth," by *There are no hills to climb, no streams to ford, no depths to reach.*

_____

_____

_____

_____

_____

_____

1.11 Read the poem "Lost Youth," and explain two meanings for the line: And no birds sing! Discuss the poem with your teacher or a friend.

_____

_____

_____

_____

_____

_____

Interview a person who is over sixty years old, and write down your observations.

1.12 Observe their personality, interests, and attitude toward life. Why can a person seem young at seventy or eighty?

_____

_____

_____

_____

_____

_____

_____

_____

_____

_____

TEACHER CHECK _____ _____

initials   date

Write out the meanings of the following vocabulary words. You will be tested on the definitions.

1.13 emphasis _____

1.14 knots _____

1.15 drowsily _____

1.16 sated _____

1.17 legendary _____

1.18 repetition _____

1.19 economy _____

Select the vocabulary words that will correctly answer the following statements.

1.20 _____ After a gigantic meal, you feel this way.

1.21 _____ Never wasteful.

1.22 _____ Beowulf is this type of hero.

WORD INFLECTIONS

Many new words are formed from familiar words by just adding a syllable or changing a letter in the known word. These changes are called _inflectional changes_. You will find it easier to remember the meaning and spelling of certain words by knowing the base word it comes from – for example, an inflectional form of the word _habit_ would be _habitual_. (Note: habit is a noun, habitual is an adjective). When you add a prefix or a suffix, you are making an inflectional change.

 Look in the dictionary and find an inflectional form of each of the following words.
Note: Most related words are placed together in alphabetical order.

1.23 a. break _____

b. elephant _____

c. error _____

d. escape _____

e. flirt _____

f. globe _____

g. herb _____

h. infant   _____

i. note   _____

j. part   _____

k. pilgrim   _____

l. real   _____

m. type   _____

n. recommend   _____

Write the meanings of the following vocabulary words. Learn these meanings, because you will be using them.

1.24 chant _____

1.25 monotonous _____

1.26 constrain _____

1.27 pliant _____

1.28 formal _____

1.29 epic _____

1.30 ford _____

Complete the sentences using the vocabulary words you defined in the preceding exercise.

1.31 The soldiers tried to _____ the river.

1.32 When we write our schoolwork, we use _____ grammar.

1.33 The long poem about Hiawatha is an _____ poem.

1.34 The singer had a(n) _____ voice.

1.35 The reed was so _____ that the wind could bend it.

1.36 The chorus _____ the song.

WORD VARIATIONS

The English language is made more interesting because many common objects have different names for the same thing. These differences are due to the variety of countries and regions that speak the same language. For example, a living room is also a drawing room, a sitting room, a front room, or a parlor. Words that mean the same thing are synonyms.

The creative use of synonyms is one way to make thoughts and words sound fresh and new.

Complete each sentence with a different name for each underlined word.

1.37 The <u>skin</u> of an animal is a h _____ .

1.38 A <u>rug</u> can also be called a c _____ .

1.39 A <u>divan</u> is also called a c _____ or a s _____ .

1.40 A <u>roasted turkey leg</u> is also called a d _____ .

1.41 An <u>arm</u> or a <u>leg</u> is also called a l _____ .

1.42 The <u>top of your head</u> is called the c _____ .

1.43 Your <u>digits</u> are also called fingers and t _____ .

Hunt the words. Be a detective and find the hidden words in the poem "Best of Two Worlds." The hidden word may be part of one or two words. Write the word(s) from the poem and circle the hidden word. You will be given a clue.

(Clue) Another word for boy: b a l (l a d)

1.44 (Clue) Opposite of old: _____

1.45 (Clue) Past tense of eat: _____

1.46 (Clue) Name for a direction: _____

1.47 (Clue) Name of a president of the United States: _____

1.48 (Clue) Inside: _____

1.49 (Clue) To be conscious of: _____

1.50 (Clue) A person: _____

1.51 (Clue) Birds have these: _____

1.52 (Clue) The next in line to a throne: _____

1.53 (Clue) Something to catch fish with: _____

Unscramble the following words. They are all to be found in the poem "Fish."

1.54 a. twah   _____

       b. erhit   _____

       c. erseh   _____

       d. dsleab   _____

       e. gshutoht   _____

       f. npialt   _____

       g. tonsk   _____

       h. gldheti   _____

SPELLING AND HANDWRITING

Eleven of the spelling words in this section contain a general pattern (*-mit, -mote*), and the rest are homonyms. You will find it easier to spell words if you recognize existing patterns.

Spelling. Your handwriting practice is with all lowercase letters that start counter-clockwise.

Learn to spell the words from Spelling Words-1.

SPELLING WORDS-1

admit	submit	bail	boll
commit	demote	bale	choir
emit	mote	board	quire
omit	promote	bored	cue
permit	remote	bole	queue
remit			

Notice that *sub-*, *ad-*, *per-*, *re-*, and *pro-* are common *prefixes* that have a particular meaning when added to a word.

 Copy the spelling words in your best handwriting, placing them all in alphabetical order.

1.55 a. _____   b. _____

c. _____   d. _____

e. _____   f. _____

g. _____   h. _____

i. _____   j. _____

k. _____   l. _____

m. _____   n. _____

o. _____   p. _____

q. _____   r. _____

s. _____   t. _____

u. _____

Use your dictionary to find the meanings of the following spelling words.

1.56 omit _____

1.57 submit _____

1.58 remit _____

1.59 emit _____

1.60 demote _____

1.61 remote _____

1.62 mote _____

1.63 bole _____

1.64 bale _____

1.65 quire _____

Match the following spelling words with their meanings.

1.66	_____	demote	a.	a particle of dust
1.67	_____	quire	b.	leave out
1.68	_____	mote	c.	distant
1.69	_____	submit	d.	the trunk of a tree
1.70	_____	omit	e.	to lower in rank or position
1.71	_____	bole	f.	a large bundle of goods
1.72	_____	bale	g.	twenty-five sheets of paper (same kind)
			h.	to surrender or yield

Handwriting. Notice that the small letters *o, c, a, d, g,* and *q* all start counter-clockwise, that is, they all start with a downward stroke to the left. Remember to keep all your lowercase letters exactly the same height.

Copy these words three times.

1.73

occasion   good   squad   ghost

Ask your teacher to give you a practice spelling test of Spelling Words-1. Restudy the words you missed.

Review the material in this section in preparation for the Self Test. This Self Test will check your mastery of this particular section. The items missed on this Self Test will indicate specific areas where restudy is needed for mastery.

SELF TEST 1

Match these items by writing the correct letter in the blank (each answer, 2 points).

1.01 _____ pattern

1.02 _____ a story poem

1.03 _____ a poem that does not follow any strict pattern

1.04 _____ an addition or change made to a word

1.05 _____ stanza

1.06 _____ rhythm

1.07 _____ an epic poem

a. involves a legendary hero

b. inflectional change

c. beat

d. rhyme

e. repetition planned for an effect

f. narrative poem

g. a verse

h. free verse

Write the words to match the definition (each answer, 3 points).

1.08 A long poem of adventures. _____

1.09 Bending easily. _____

1.010 A measurement used to tell how far a ship has traveled. _____

1.011 Boring because it is always the same. _____

1.012 Another word for sleepy. _____

Complete these sentences (each answer, 3 points).

1.013 Another name for a couch is a _____ .

1.014 Yet another name for a couch is a _____ .

1.015 Your legs and arms are called _____ .

1.016 Fingers and toes are called _____ .

1.017 The skin of an animal is also called _____ .

Write the correct word in each blank to complete the following sentences (each answer, 3 points).

admit	emit	permit	remote
commit	mote	promote	submit
demote	omit	remit	

1.018 The teacher _____ ted telling me that I had failed the test.

1.019 I _____ I did not try very hard.

1.020 I had to _____ two book reports in order to pass.

1.021 The teacher did not _____ me to go on the field trip.

1.022 I live in a(n) _____ area, very far from town.

1.023 Smoke and flames started to _____ from the dragon's nose.

1.024 It is unfair to _____ the colonel in the army to the rank of private.

1.025 The pirate was put in prison for _____ ting a crime.

What are the four major characteristics of poetry (each answer, 3 points)?

1.026 _____

1.027 _____

1.028 _____

1.029 _____

Answer these questions about the poems in Section One (each answer, 4 points).

1.030 Were the lines in the poem, "Fish," rhymed or unrhymed?

_____

1.031 Did all of the three poems in Section One have rhythm? _____

1.032 What two worlds did the birds on the telephone wire make the best of?

_____

_____

1.033 Why did the man in the poem, "Lost Youth," seem old at thirty?

_____

_____

1.034 Why is the use of synonyms helpful in creative writing?

_____

_____

80 / 100   **SCORE** _____   **TEACHER** _____ _____
                                                        initials   date

ABC   **Take your spelling test of Spelling Words-1.**

2. SECTION TWO

This section will give you some understanding of the need for vivid and descriptive words in poetry, and will help you explore the use of similes, metaphors, and alliteration. You will discuss forced rhyme and invented words. You will learn more homonyms and pattern words and practice handwriting.

Section Objectives

Review these objectives. When you have completed this section, you should be able to:

1. Identify certain poetic styles.
2. Write poems of your own, using some of the poetic forms studied in this LIFEPAC.
4. Identify effective rhyme and word choice.
5. Demonstrate economy of words in writing poetry.
6. Identify alliteration, similes, and metaphors.
9. Spell and use some new homonyms.
10. Identify patterns in words.
11. Write the definitions of some vocabulary words.
12. Identify sounds and their various spellings.
13. Use a basic vocabulary of literary terms.

Vocabulary

Study these words to enhance your learning success in this section.

alliteration (u lit′ u rā ′ shun). The repetition of the same letter at the beginning of two or more words in sequence.

brilliant (bril′ yunt). Having great ability.

bristle (bris′ ul). To stand up straight; have one's hair stand up straight.

category (kat′ e gôr ē). A division, species, or group.

cliché (klē shā′). An overused idea or expression.

knack (nak). The ability or power to do something easily; special skill.

mood (müd). A state of mind or feeling.

selective (si lekt′ uv). Making a choice among several.

wooden (wu d un). Stiff as wood; dull; stupid.

Pronunciation Key: hat, āge, cãre, fär; let, ēqual, tėrm; it, īce; hot, ōpen, ôrder; oil; out; cup, pút, rüle; child; long; thin; /ℱH/ for then; /zh/ for measure; /u/ or /ə/ represents /a/ in about, /e/ in taken, /i/ in pencil, /o/ in lemon, and /u/ in circus.

FIGURES OF SPEECH

Because a poet uses so few words, they have to be very **selective** in their choice of words. To be selective they must also have a large vocabulary from which to choose. The poet needs to choose vivid, descriptive words in order to paint a clear "word-picture." You, too, will be writing poetry by the end of this LIFEPAC.

You will try some exercises to help you build a store of usable words.

First, find words to suit certain **moods**. Use your dictionary, a dictionary of synonyms, or a thesaurus (word finder). The thesaurus will be the most helpful because it sorts words into **categories**.

Write at least five words for each mood (more if you can). You may use a dictionary or another word finder.

2.1 Quiet words: (murmur, softly)

_____

_____

2.2 Noisy words: (crack, splash)

_____

_____

2.3 Slow words: (immovable, elephant)

_____

_____

2.4 Quick words: (skip, dash)

_____

_____

Notice that hard sounds (like /t/, /g/, /d/, /b/) give a noisy, quick feeling; soft sounds (like /s/, /l/, /f/, /m/) give a gentle, quiet, or slow feeling.

Make a list of words to match the following categories.

2.5 Words to describe pleasant smells:

_____

_____

2.6 Words to describe shiny objects:

_____

_____

2.7 Sound words that explode, like "pop":

_____

_____

2.8 Sound animal noises, like "squeak":

_____

_____

Write sentences that describe each of the following phrases. Use words from the lists you have made.

2.9 The sound of a typewriter: _____

_____

2.10 The look of a beetle's back: _____

_____

2.11 The smell of autumn: _____

_____

TEACHER CHECK _____ _____
                              initials   date

Similes. In Language Arts LIFEPAC 601, you learned about *hyperbole*, which is a figure of speech. A simile is also a figure of speech. The word *simile* comes from the Latin word *similis* meaning *like* (or similar). When you use a simile, you are comparing things or saying that something is like something else.

The angry cat's back **bristled** *like a hairbrush*.

The simile *like a hairbrush* gives you an exact mental picture of how the cat looked when it was angry.

Here is another familiar simile:

A jet travels *as fast as a speeding bullet*.

Similes are useful and very colorful when used in poetry. However, similes can become **clichés** because they are used too often. When something becomes a cliché, it tends to be boring. When you write your own poems, try to be imaginative and think up new similes. Some cliché similes are as *easy as pie, as quick as a wink*, or *as smart as a whip*. Notice the *as...as* form.

Similes often begin with the clue words *like...*, *than..., as...as,* or *so...as*.

Finish the following cliché similes.

2.12 as white as s _____

2.13 as white as a s _____

2.14 as sweet as h _____

2.15 as sly as a f _____

2.16 as pretty as a p _____

2.17 as right as r _____

2.18 as busy as a b _____

2.19 as black as n _____

2.20 as fast as the w _____

Make up some similes of your own which are unusual, not clichés.

2.21 The sun was as hot as _____ .

2.22 The lion was fierce like _____ .

2.23 My head felt like _____ .

2.24 The old house looked like _____ .

2.25 The sea was as smooth as _____ .

2.26 The tank crossed the field like _____ .

Review the meanings of the following vocabulary words; then match the words with their definitions.

2.27 _____ knack

2.28 _____ mood

2.29 _____ bristle

2.30 _____ selective

2.31 _____ cliché

2.32 _____ brilliant

2.33 _____ compress

a. choosy

b. squeeze together

c. splendid

d. the ability to do something

e. to rise or stand stiff with anger

f. a particular state of mind or feeling

g. passing quickly

h. a word or phrase used too often

Metaphors. Like similes, metaphors are figures of speech. Both techniques help a poet or writer paint a clearer picture by comparing things. Where a simile only says a thing is like something else, a metaphor says one thing is something else.

My mother is a peach.

This expression means she is as sweet and lovely as a peach.

I am a tiger when it comes to work.

This expression means I am as strong and energetic as a tiger when I work.

In these two examples of metaphors, notice how you do not use the clue words *like* or *as... as*, as you would with a simile. Here the helper verbs *is* and *am* are used.

 Turn back to Section One of this LIFEPAC and reread the poem "Fish."
Write two metaphors that stand for "fish."

2.34 Five-word phrase _____ _____ _____ _____ _____

2.35 Four-word phrase _____ _____ _____ _____

Metaphors can also be clichés. We use them in our speech all the time. Some can even be grouped, there are so many of them. We will look at two large groups of metaphors–those using color words, and those using body parts.

Complete the following group of color cliché metaphors.
Use these color names: black, blue, red, gold, green, yellow, purple, and white.

2.36 It was a _____ letter day for me.

2.37 I go to the doctor once in a _____ moon.

2.38 He is the _____ sheep of the family.

2.39 The boy was _____ with envy.

2.40 The book was pure _____ it was so expensive.

2.41 The man was _____ with rage.

2.42 After the accident, the day was _____ for everyone.

2.43 My sister was _____ from the motion of the boat.

2.44 Our company's finances were in the _____ .

2.45 The children were good as _____ .

A large group of cliché metaphors refer to parts of the body.

Examples	Meaning
Keep a stiff upper lip.	Be brave.
She has a finger in every pie.	She is involved in everything.
He said a mouthful.	He spoke at great length, or said a lot.

Explain what the following body metaphors mean.

2.46 I got an earful: _____

_____

2.47 To put your foot in your mouth: _____

_____

2.48 Don't lose your head: _____

_____

2.49 To see eye to eye: _____

_____

2.50 To get it off your chest: _____

_____

2.51 To put your nose to the grindstone: _____

_____

2.52 To stick your neck out: _____

_____

Complete this activity.

2.53 As a special project, select three of the metaphors and illustrate them. Do the illustrations on another sheet of paper or in the space below.

TEACHER CHECK _____ _____
                              initials   date

Complete the crossword puzzle.

2.54   Most of these clues are metaphors.

Across

1. A pain in the n _____
3. A f _____ in every pie
7. This _____ that
8. To get an e _____
11. As slippery as an _____
13. Keep your _____ up (means be cheerful)
14. As big as a b _____
15. Opposite of out
16. a green light says this
18. Seat minus s
20. A common suffix
21. As dead as a d _____ (an extinct bird)
24. Another word for smell
26. Opposite of over
30. Opposite of B.C.
31. An Egyptian dried fruit

Down

2. See _____ to eye
4. A negative word
5. _____ with envy
6. To get things r _____
9. A letter of certain ancient alphabets (rhymes with tune)
10. Last but not l _____
12. To break the i _____ (to get things going)
15. A part of pin
16. As _____ as gold
17. Peculiar
19. Abbreviation for Automobile Association
22. A sound of admiration
23. San + d — s
25. Name of the sun god in ancient Egypt
27. Abbreviation for a district attorney
28. Latin for *and*
29. Royal Eggplant (an abbreviation)

POETIC DEVICES

A poet plays with words as a child plays with blocks, building a special picture that pleases the eye, ear, and mind. **Alliteration**, rhyming, forced rhyme, and invented words are just four ways of playing with words.

Alliteration. The early Anglo-Saxon poets in England enjoyed using a poetic device called *alliteration*. They either made the beginning letters all the same or the vowel sounds all the same. "Many muddle-headed men murmured in the meadows." Here, the letter *m* is repeated five times. This sentence is an example of alliteration.

 Circle the words in the following sentences that show alliteration.

2.55 Our shy, young sister Suzy is sewing shirts for soldiers.

2.56 A devastatingly debonair dandy dawdled down the drive.

2.57 Toss Tom the tissue, Terry.

Write the alliterative words. Turn back to the first section to read the poems again.

2.58 Words in the poem "Fish" that have the /s/ sound at the beginning.

_____

2.59 Words in the first two lines of "Best of Two Worlds" that have the /w/ sound at the beginning.

_____

2.60 Words in last two lines of "Best of Two Worlds" that have the /d/ sound at the beginning.

_____

A fourteenth-century poem (one of the earliest known in English literature) begins like this.

"Swart, sweaty smiths, smutched
with smoke,
Drive me to death with din of their
dints."*

*dints means blows

Notice the repetition of *sw* and *sm* in the first line and the letter *d* in the second line. These lines show how alliteration uses the repetition of a letter or a sound in a sentence.

Rhyming. Rhyme is the repetition of end sounds. In thirteenth-century England there lived a **brilliant** poet named Geoffrey Chaucer, whose most famous work is called *The Canterbury Tales*. In his day it was popular to have poems rhyme in couplets — every two lines ended with a rhyming word. In the next section of this LIFEPAC, you will learn about rhyming patterns.

Forced Rhyme. Rhyming can be clever if it fits naturally into the mood of the poem and if the choice of rhyme is imaginative. However, nothing is worse than forced rhyme. Forced rhyme sounds unnatural.

Here is an example of a forced rhyme.

> A very fat cat
> Sat on a mat,
> Eating a rat,
> In his best Sunday hat!

There is nothing clever or imaginative about these four lines. The end words rhyme only because they were made to rhyme, not because they were the best words that could be found.

Make up each sentence with as many words that rhyme with the given clue word.
You will be given a clue.

Example: tin

The thin man of tin
Had dirt on his chin;
He said with a grin:
"The dirt matches my shirt!"

2.61 (Clue) call: _____

_____

_____

2.62 (Clue) fight: _____

_____

_____

Notice how you had to force your rhyme. Forced rhyme makes your words seem **wooden** or unimaginative.

Invented words. A poet often invents words to add humor to their poetry. A popular author of children's books is Dr. Seuss, who has written such books as *The Cat in the Hat*, *The Lorax*, and *The Grinch Who Stole Christmas*. He has the clever **knack** of inventing words and creatures that are very funny, and he uses forced rhyme very effectively.

Complete the following activities.

Independent research: Look up any Dr. Seuss book in your library and write the following information.

2.63 a. The title: _____

b. Author: _____

c. Publisher: _____

2.64 Some invented words used in the book that you particularly like are:

_____

_____

2.65 The funniest stanza (or verse) in the book, in your opinion is:

_____

_____

_____

_____

2.66 Write a short, funny story using invented words for as many things as you can. Pretend you are in a world that has animals, birds, trees, useful tools, and people that have never been seen before and you have to invent names for all of them. Notice how peculiar it all sounds.

Write your story on a separate sheet of paper. Ask your teacher to allow you to read it aloud to the class.

TEACHER CHECK _____ _____
                      initials   date

SPELLING AND HANDWRITING

Your spelling words again show a pattern. Your handwriting practice is on the capital letters *P*, *B*, and *R*.

Spelling. Remember, recognizing patterns in words helps you with the spelling. The two patterns here are *-itude* and *para-*. You will also learn more homonyms.

Learn to spell the words from Spelling Words-2.

SPELLING WORDS-2

gait	morn	altitude	fortitude	parakeet
gate	mourn	aptitude	multitude	parallel
miner	serf	attitude	parable	paramedic
minor	surf	beatitude	parachute	parasol

Copy the spelling words in your best handwriting, placing them in alphabetical order.

2.67 a. _____ b. _____

c. _____ d. _____

e. _____ f. _____

g. _____ h. _____

i. _____ j. _____

k. _____ l. _____

m. _____ n. _____

o. _____ p. _____

q. _____ r. _____

s. _____ t. _____

Use the dictionary to find the meanings of the following spelling words.

2.68 multitude _____

2.69 altitude _____

2.70 aptitude _____

2.71 fortitude _____

2.72 parable _____

2.73 parasol _____

2.74 beatitude _____

2.75 attitude _____

2.76 parallel _____

Use spelling words from Spelling Words-2 to complete the following sentences.

2.77 Jesus fed the _____ with only a few loaves and fishes.

2.78 Jesus talked to people in _____ so that they could understand his teachings better.

2.79 A jet plane has to fly at a very high _____ .

2.80 The woman carried a _____ to protect herself from the sun.

2.81 A section of Jesus' teachings in the New Testament is called the _____ .

Match the following words with their definitions. Look up the meanings first.

2.82 _____ surf

2.83 _____ gate

2.84 _____ minor

2.85 _____ morn

2.86 _____ serf

2.87 _____ gait

2.88 _____ miner

2.89 _____ mourn

a. fine green grass

b. poetic word for morning

c. a digger for buried rock

d. a manner of walking

e. to cry with grief

f. smaller or less (a person under eighteen)

g. breaking waves on the shore

h. a slave or servant in olden times

i. a barrier

ABC **Ask your teacher to give you a practice spelling test of Spelling Words-2.** Restudy the words you missed.

Handwriting. The capital letters *P*, *B*, and *R* are similar because they all begin with the same up-down strokes. Concentrate on keeping your letters on the line, with tall letters (like *b*, *l*, and *t*) having straight backs and the same height.

 Copy each of these words twice.

2.90

Bobby   Robert   Pebble   Bottle

↺ **Review the material in this section in preparation for the Self Test.** This Self Test will check your understanding of this section as well as your knowledge of the previous section.

SELF TEST 2

Circle the part of each sentence that contains similes (each answer, 2 points).

2.01   He fought like a lion.

2.02   He came home in a temper.

2.03   He ran down the hill like lightning.

2.04   He snored as loud as a tractor.

2.05   She came into the room with a smile on her face.

2.06   He turned as white as paper when he saw the accident.

2.07   She was as sweet as honey afterwards.

2.08   The goat had eyes as black as night.

Match these metaphors (each answer, 2 points).

2.09   _____   to keep a stiff upper lip   a.   to be cheerful

2.010   _____   to see eye to eye   b.   to be very angry

2.011   _____   the black sheep of a family   c.   an occasion to remember

2.012   _____   a red-letter day   d.   a nuisance

2.013   _____   keep your chin up   e.   to be brave

2.014   _____   a pain in the neck   f.   a disaster

2.015   _____   purple with rage   g.   an outcast or rebel

                                                       h.   to agree with

LANGUAGE ARTS 606

LIFEPAC TEST

NAME _____

DATE _____

SCORE _____

LANGUAGE ARTS 606: LIFEPAC TEST

Write the correct homonym in each blank to complete these sentences (each answer, 3 points).

gambol	cannon	gamble	waive
climb	wave	canon	clime
soul	sole		

1. He was the _____ person in the building.

2. The blast of the _____ shook the building.

3. Australia has a most unusual _____ .

4. Please _____ to me when you leave.

5. It is foolhardy to _____ because you could lose everything.

6. Jesus died to save your _____ .

7. The law of the church is called the _____ .

8. My friend decided to _____ my debt to him.

9. Young lambs love to _____ in springtime.

10. I would like to _____ Mount Everest.

Match the words with their meanings (each answer, 2 points).

11. _____ chant   a. special skill

12. _____ emphasis   b. easy to bend

13. _____ ford   c. doing again

14. _____ pliant   d. said it is untrue

15. _____ sated   e. stand up straight

16. _____ repetition   f. stress

17. _____ knack   g. measurement of speed

18. _____ brilliant   h. to cross a river

19. _____ denial   i. to stop someone

20. _____ knot   j. to sing

21. _____ waylay   k. full and satisfied

22. _____ monotonous   l. boring

                                        m. having great ability

Explain these terms and give an example of each (each answer, 5 points).

23.   palindrome _____

        _____

24.   metaphor _____

        _____

25.   acronym _____

        _____

Complete these statements (each answer, 3 points).

26.   "Silver light" and "sheer delight" from the poem "Fish" are an example of effective

        _____ .

27.   Economy of words and rhythm are two major characteristics of

        _____ .

28.   The pattern in the words *altitude* and *attitude* is _____ .

29.   A new word made from the word *break* by adding an inflectional change is

        _____ .

30.   A new word made from the word *pilgrim* by adding an inflectional change is

        _____ .

Match the term with the description (each answer, 2 points).

31.   _____ an epic poem

32.   _____ thesaurus

33.   _____ dialogue

34.   _____ minstrel

35.   _____ lullaby

36.   _____ free verse

37.   _____ limerick

38.   _____ ballad

a. conversation

b. poetry that does not have a formal pattern

c. a story poem, often written to be sung

d. a gentle, soft song

e. a traveling entertainer

f. the story of "Beowulf"

g. a dictionary that is categorized

h. a mythical beast

i. a five-lined, clever, and funny poem with certain lines rhyming

Take your LIFEPAC Spelling Test.

Complete the sentences using these words (each sentence, 4 points). Some words may be used more than once.

altitude	fortitude	parakeet
aptitude	multitude	parallel
attitude	parable	paramedic
beatitude	parachute	parasol

2.016 The a. _____ of people held b. _____ s to protect themselves from the sun.

2.017 The pilot could not a. _____ at that b. _____ .

2.018 Jesus told some beautiful a. _____ to the b. _____ .

2.019 The a. _____ raced to the disaster scene to give first-aid to a flock of b. _____ .

2.020 The a. _____ did not make its descent in a b. _____ line to the tall building.

2.021 "Your a. _____ is very good, and I see you have an b. _____ for mathematics," said the teacher.

2.022 A a. _____ could not fly to that high b. _____ .

2.023 I face the terrifying interview with much a. _____ because I wanted to get the job as a b. _____ .

Match these terms/names with their definitions (each answer, 2 points).

2.024 _____ thesaurus

2.025 _____ cliché

2.026 _____ simile

2.027 _____ metaphor

2.028 _____ alliteration

2.029 _____ Geoffrey Chaucer

2.030 _____ couplet

2.031 _____ Dr. Seuss

a. a two-line poem

b. a figure of speech that says one thing is the same as another

c. a children's author

d. a kind of dictionary

e. free verse

f. as... as (form of comparison)

g. an overused expression

h. repetition of a letter beginning each word in a sequence

i. the author of "The Canterbury Tales"

Answer true or false (each answer, 1 point).

2.032 _____ A stanza is a type of music.

2.033 _____ A narrative poem has a very narrow form.

2.034 _____ Inflectional changes involve adding letters or endings to base words.

2.035 _____ Free verse is written by free men.

2.036 _____ An epic poem tells the story of a legendary hero.

2.037 _____ A knot is a measurement of speed.

2.038 _____ A digit is a form of midget.

2.039 _____ A drawing room is a bedroom.

2.040 _____ Poor rhythm can be monotonous.

2.041 _____ Rhythm can be described as stress or emotional emphasis.

Circle the inflectional endings of each word, and write the ending on the line (each answer, 2 points).

2.042 breakable _____   **2.045** notation _____

2.043 herbal _____   **2.046** infantile _____

2.044 pilgrimage _____   **2.047** elephantine _____

80 / 100   **SCORE** _____   **TEACHER** _____ _____
                                                        initials   date

ABC **Take your spelling test of Spelling Words-2.**

3. SECTION THREE

This section will show you that poetry can take many shapes and forms. You will be exposed to pen pictures, Ezra Pound couplets, Dylan Thomas couplets, cinquains, and shaped poems.

Section Objectives

Review these objectives. When you have finished this section, you should be able to:

1. Identify certain poetic styles.
2. Write poems of your own, using some of the poetic forms studied in this LIFEPAC.
3. List some of the major characteristics of poetry.
4. Identify effective rhyme and word choice.
5. Demonstrate economy of words in writing poetry.
7. Write acronyms.
9. Spell and use some new homonyms.
11. Write the definitions of some vocabulary words.
12. Identify sounds and their various spellings.
13. Use a basic vocabulary of literary terms.

Vocabulary

Study these words to enhance your learning success in this section.

emphasize (em' fu sīz). Put special stress on.

incorporate (in kôr' pu rā t). To make something a part of something else.

sift (sift). To let fall through (or as if through) a sieve.

spectator (spek' tā tur). A person who looks on without taking part.

tantalizing (tan' tu līz ing). Tempting; teasing; very desirable but out of reach.

tasteful (tāst' ful). Done in good taste.

tenacious (ti nā' shus). Holding fast; stubborn.

topsy-turvy (top' sē ter' vē). Upside down; in confusion and disorder.

turbulent (tèr' byu lunt). Disorderly; violent; greatly disturbed.

Pronunciation Key: hat, āge, cãre, fär; let, ēqual, tèrm; it, īce; hot, ōpen, ôrder; oil; out; cup, pu̇t, rüle; child; long; thin; /ᵵH/ for then; /zh/ for measure; /u/ or /ə/ represents /a/ in about, /e/ in taken, /i/ in pencil, /o/ in lemon, and /u/ in circus.

POETIC FORMS

In Section One, you learned that a major characteristic of poetry is pattern. The pattern might be in the shape of the poem, when and where you use rhyme, the length of each line, or the rhythm that is selected. Now let us look at some poetic forms and notice the line and verse patterns that the poets use.

Pen pictures. A pen picture is a very short, three-lined poem, each line being a metaphor (description) of the subject of the poem.

Here are three pen pictures by Annis Mather. Read the poems carefully and see how each metaphor adds meaning to the subject of the poem.

"Children's Laughter"

Red apples spilling from a basket,
Golden sand **sifted** through the fingers,
Stream-water dripping over a stone.

"Youth"

Ivy climbing over a wall,
Salmon leaping in mid-stream,
A terrier barking at an elephant.

"Old Age"

Travelers waiting for a train,
Runners resting after a race,
Spectators watching a pageant.

-Annis Mather

Notice how the poet, Annis Mather, pictures laughter as movement with the word phrases *rolling* apples, *sifting* sand, *dripping* water. We know that laughter is not really these things, but by using them as metaphors, the term *children's laughter* becomes more meaningful to us. As in a painting, these colorful images **emphasize** the meaning of laughter.

Write your own pen picture.

Pick a subject (something fairly easy and familiar to you, for example, brothers, my sister, lost puppy) and write a pen picture of your own. Reread Section Two's discussion on metaphors, if you need help. Share your pen picture with a friend.

3.1   (subject) _____

Write three vivid metaphors.

_____

_____

_____

FRIEND'S CHECK _____ _____
                     initials   date

Ezra Pound couplets. Another poetic form for you to try is called the *Ezra Pound couplet* (a couplet means two lines). Ezra Pound was a famous American poet. One night, while standing in a subway exit watching people come up out of the underground darkness into the brightly-lit streets, he wrote a two-line poem describing the experience. To him, the pale faces of the crowd against the darkness of the exit way, looked like flower petals on a "wet, black bough."

His first line stated what he saw (the crowd exiting from the subway); his second line was a metaphor (what the crowd appeared to be–petals on a bough).

When you write your own couplet, remember to ask yourself what your subject reminds you of. This will help you write your own metaphor for the second line. For example, you might see a "freeway full of cars," and feel that it looks like "an army of slow-moving ants."

 Select your own metaphors to complete each of the following couplets. Remember to ask yourself what each reminds you of. Share these couplets with your teacher.

3.2   An acrobat swinging through the air,

_____

3.3   An old oak tree struck by lightning,

_____

3.4   A submarine patrolling the seas,

_____

3.5   A cat, hunched up, spitting in rage,

_____

Dylan Thomas couplets. This form of couplet is to be found frequently in the poetry of a Welsh poet named Dylan Thomas. The first line is in the form of a question; the second line (or answer) is composed of four made-up adjectives.

    Did you ever see an eagle?

    Brave-hearted, strong-winged, wind-borne, sky-free.

Notice that the adjectives are hyphenated. By using these hyphens, the poet has turned an adjective and a noun into a double-barreled adjective.

For example:

Adjective	Noun	New Adjective
fierce	face	= fierce-faced
blue	shadows	= blue-shadowed
wild	eyes	= wild-eyed

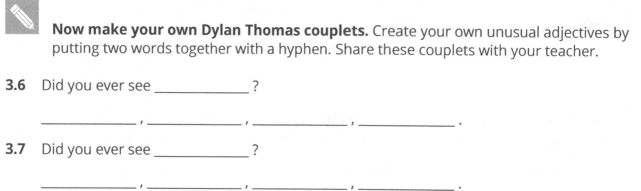

Now make your own Dylan Thomas couplets. Create your own unusual adjectives by putting two words together with a hyphen. Share these couplets with your teacher.

3.6   Did you ever see _____ ?

_____ , _____ , _____ , _____ .

3.7   Did you ever see _____ ?

_____ , _____ , _____ , _____ .

Cinquains. A cinquain (sing kaen) is a five-line poem, with a set number of words in each line, and a certain kind of word in each line. The French word *cinq* means *five*, which is why it is called a cinquain.

Here is an example.

> Apples,
> Rosy, juicy,
> Sweet, delicious, crisp,
> Better still in pies,
> Apples.

Notice the form (or pattern) of a cinquain. The first and fifth line is repeated and states the topic of the poem. The second line has two adjectives; the third line has three adjectives; and the fourth line is a phrase (not a complete sentence) consisting of four words.

Try to write your own cinquain. Remember to select adjectives that describe sight, sound, taste, smell and touch. These will help develop a stronger picture of what you are describing.

Write a cinquain of your own.

3.8 (subject) _____

(two adjectives) _____ , _____ ,

(three adjectives) _____ , _____ , _____ ,

(phrase of four words) _____ ,

(repeat subject) _____ .

TEACHER CHECK _____ _____
                    initials   date

Shaped poems. A shaped poem involves the use of a page pattern. A shaped poem is put together in the form of a picture. If the poem is about a snake, the words are put together in the shape of a snake.

The following poem uses words beginning with the letter *T*; its shape is also in the form of a capital *T*. The poem plays with words and the way words sound. It does not have to make sense. It is just for fun.

A "T" is terrific, when said with a drawl, **tantalizing**, **tasteful** —

it stands, straight and tall, for

tables,

tentacles,

and

tugs;

tenacious,

threadbare,

and

topsy-turvy

slugs;

teacups,

tortoises,

turbulent,

toes;

my list of

"T" words

just

grows

and

grows!

Notice that the nonsense poem uses the pattern or shape of the letter *T*, and **incorporates** as many words beginning with *T* as seems best.

The famous English author, Lewis Carroll, who wrote the book *Alice in Wonderland* was a master at making up puzzles, jokes, riddles, and word plays. The following exercise will help you to know Lewis Carroll better, and show you a clever "shaped poem."

 Complete these activities.

Individual Research. Select any edition of "Alice in Wonderland" to be found in the library. Turn to Chapter 3, and read about the mouse's tale. You can also find this chapter online.

3.9 What page is the shaped poem on? _____

3.10 What shape did the poem take? _____

3.11 What are the words Carroll chose to rhyme with these words?

    a. mouse   _____

    b. denial   _____

    c. cur   _____

    d. breath   _____

    e. jury   _____

3.12 Why did Alice think that the mouse's tale took such a funny shape? _____

_____

_____

Write a shaped poem.

3.13 Using your own initial, either first or last, write a short shaped poem. Use as many words as you can that begin with your initial. Write your poem on an extra sheet of paper and decorate it as imaginatively as possible. Save it to put in the book of poetry which you will make.

TEACHER CHECK _____ _____

                                                             initials   date

SHORTENED FORMS OF WORDS

All shortened forms are used for convenience and speed. The term U.S.A. is certainly quicker to say and to write than the *United States of America.* Saying the whole title or word sounds more grand and poetic, but for everyday speech and writing, people tend to contract, abbreviate, or make acronyms.

Abbreviated words. In Language Arts LIFEPAC 605 some abbreviations were studied as spelling words. These abbreviations were the kind which are followed by a period. Another kind of shortened word is not followed by a period. Many of these shortened forms are "slang" words, but many have been accepted as informal English.

Examples: auto for automobile
bike for bicycle
math for mathematics

 Match the following shortened words with the full base word.

3.14	_____	varsity	a.	Yankee
3.15	_____	mike	b.	influenza
3.16	_____	isle	c.	caravan
3.17	_____	mum	d.	convict
3.18	_____	flu	e.	university
3.19	_____	scram	f.	quiet
3.20	_____	van	g.	lubricating oil
3.21	_____	Yank	h.	microphone
3.22	_____	con	i.	chrysanthemum
3.23	_____	lube	j.	island
			k.	scramble

Acronyms. Another group of shortened words is called acronyms. An acronym is usually formed from the first letters or syllable of a compound term, phrase, name, or title.

For example *NATO* stands for *North Atlantic Treaty Organization.*

Here are some acronyms you should learn: radar, scuba, ZIP, sonar, HUD, and NASA.

Match the following acronyms with the word phrases they stand for. Use an unabridged dictionary if necessary.

3.24 _____ sound navigation ranging

3.25 _____ Zoning Improvement Plan (postal department)

3.26 _____ radio detecting and ranging

3.27 _____ National Aeronautics and Space Administration

3.28 _____ self-contained underwater breathing apparatus

3.29 _____ Housing and Urban Development

a. scuba

b. HUD

c. sonar

d. NASA

e. CETA

f. radar

g. ZIP

Notice how the acronyms were formed by the first letter or syllable of each word. These acronyms are continually used in our daily speech and writing because they are easier to say than the original title.

SPELLING AND HANDWRITING

The spelling words are all homonyms. For handwriting, you will practice more capital letters.

Spelling. Learn the words in Spelling Words-3, which are all homonyms. Because homonyms sound the same, make little memory aids for yourself to help you to remember which is which.

Learn to spell the words from Spelling Words-3.

SPELLING WORDS-3

lyre	rein	peal	horde	piece	mean
lone	seam	mews	idol	reign	muse
peace	idle	mien	ale	loan	soar
ail	sore	liar	seem	hoard	peel

Copy the spelling words in your best handwriting, placing them in alphabetical order.

3.30 a. _____   b. _____

c. _____   d. _____

e. _____   f. _____

g. _____   h. _____

i. _____   j. _____

k. _____   l. _____

m. _____   n. _____

o. _____   p. _____

q. _____   r. _____

s. _____   t. _____

u. _____   v. _____

w. _____   x. _____

Use your dictionary and find the meanings of the following spelling words. Notice they are all one-syllable words.

3.31 muse _____

3.32 mews _____

3.33 mien _____

3.34 horde _____

3.35 peel _____

3.36 lone _____

3.37 lyre _____

3.38 soar _____

3.39 ale _____

3.40 ail _____

3.41 **Make a crossword puzzle.** Use six of the words in 3.31-3.40 and any other words you want. Keep it small. Write it on an extra sheet of paper, and when it is completed, give it to a friend to do for fun.

TEACHER CHECK _____ _____
                                    initials   date

ABC **Ask your teacher to give you a practice spelling test of Spelling Words-3.** Restudy the words you missed.

Handwriting. Notice that the capitals *J* and *I* start with a curved upward stroke starting from the line. The *J* finishes the down stroke below the line like a small *g*.

Copy each of these words twice.

3.42

January   I   Isaac   Judo

Review the material in this section to prepare for the Self Test. This Self Test will check your understanding of this section and will review the other sections. Any items you miss in this test will show you what areas you need to restudy.

SELF TEST 3

Write the shortened form of these words (each answer, 3 points).

3.01 _____ caravan

3.02 _____ convict

3.03 _____ island

3.04 _____ university

3.05 _____ influenza

What do these acronyms stand for (each answer, 3 points)?

3.06 ZIP _____

3.07 Sonar _____

3.08 HUD _____

3.09 NASA _____

Match these words or terms (each answer, 2 points).

3.010 _____ forced rhyme

3.011 _____ Dr. Seuss

3.012 _____ cliché

3.013 _____ narrative

3.014 _____ free verse

3.015 _____ rhythm

3.016 _____ metaphor

3.017 _____ monotonous

a. used too often

b. no formal pattern

c. word finder

d. wooden and unimaginative

e. beat, stress, or emotional emphasis

f. name for story poems

g. uses invented words

h. added suffixes

i. something is spoken of as if it were something else

j. boring

Write the correct homonym in each blank to complete these sentences (each answer, 3 points).

mien	liar	peel	horde
rein	hoard	mean	reign
peal	lone	lyre	loan

3.018 Mother asked me to _____ the potatoes.

3.019 A _____ of barbarians galloped by on horseback.

3.020 The princess picked up the _____ and began to play.

3.021 The king had a very long _____ .

3.022 The _____ survivor was finally rescued.

3.023 Standing erect he had the _____ of a statesman.

3.024 They called him a _____ , but I knew he was honest.

3.025 The pirates kept their _____ of jewels in a cave.

3.026 The rider pulled at the _____ and brought the horse to a stop.

3.027 I went to the bank for a _____ .

Complete these metaphors and similes (each numbered answer, 3 points).

3.028 To put your foot _____ _____ _____

3.029 Don't lose _____ _____

3.030 As black as _____

3.031 As good _____ _____

3.032 Put your nose _____ _____ _____

3.033 To be green _____ _____

3.034 Once in a _____ _____

Name two major characteristics of poetry (each answer, 3 points).

3.035 _____

3.036 _____

80/100 **SCORE** _____ **TEACHER** _____ _____
initials   date

ABC **Take your spelling test of Spelling Words-3.**

4. SECTION FOUR

In Sections One, Two, and Three of this LIFEPAC, you were introduced to free verse and various poetic forms, such as pen pictures, Ezra Pound couplets, Dylan Thomas couplets, cinquains, and shaped poems. In this section you will work with three more poetic forms: the **ballad**, the **limerick**, and the lullaby. You will also discuss riddles, conundrums, and palindromes, and further expand your vocabulary.

Section Objectives

Review these objectives. When you have finished this section, you should be able to:

1. Identify certain poetic styles.
2. Write poems of your own, using some of the poetic forms studied in this LIFEPAC.
3. List some of the major characteristics of poetry.
4. Identify effective rhyme and word choice.
7. Write palindromes.
9. Spell and use some new homonyms.
11. Write the definitions of some vocabulary words.
12. Identify sounds and their various spellings.
13. Use a basic vocabulary of literary terms.
14. Make an attractive book of your own poetry.

Vocabulary

Study these words to enhance your learning success in this section.

ballad (bal′ ud). A poem that tells a story in a simple verse form.

compress (kum pres′). To squeeze together; to make smaller by pressure.

dialogue (dī′ u lôg). Conversation (spoken or written out).

limerick (lim′ ur ik). A nonsense poem of five lines.

minstrel (min′ strul). A singer or musician in the Middle Ages who entertained the royalty.

mythology (mi thol′ u jē). A group of myths relating to a certain country.

rely (ri lī′). To depend on; trust.

treachery (trech′ ur ē). A breaking of faith.

waylay (wā lā′). To stop someone's travels or progress; to attack.

Pronunciation Key: hat, āge, cãre, fär; let, ēqual, tėrm; it, īce; hot, ōpen, ôrder; oil; out; cup, pùt, rüle; child; long; thin; /ŦH/ for then; /zh/ for measure; /u/ or /ə/ represents /a/ in about, /e/ in taken, /i/ in pencil, /o/ in lemon, and /u/ in circus.

MUSICAL POEMS

Ballads and lullabies were originally meant to be sung, although we often find examples of them in books of poetry.

Ballads. Hundreds of years ago, the wandering **minstrels** or storytellers were in great demand. Since there were no televisions, radios, or newspapers in those days, people **relied** on these traveling entertainers to tell them the news of the heroes and the events of the day.

A minstrel "sang for his supper" like Little Tommy Tucker. It was his way of earning his food and a place to sleep for a few nights.

The minstrel put his news into a ballad form. Often these ballads would praise the king and princes of the area, which would please those who heard them.

A ballad is a story or poem put to song.

The ballad has the following main characteristics:

1. It deals with historical events, extraordinary happenings, and heroic deeds.

2. It deals with one single scene or happening (usually an exciting or dramatic one).

3. The action is swift and **compressed**.

4. The story is told in simple language.

5. The story often deals with family relationships, romantic love, and death.

6. **Dialogue** is used.

Today we have two kinds of ballads. The *folk ballads*, whose origins are not known, have been around for hundreds of years. The *literary ballads* are written by known authors who use the folk ballad form.

Ballads, particularly the old folk ballads, usually contain dialogue. The dialogue keeps the action of the story moving. Ballads are a good example of a poet's economy with words (a characteristic of poetry). A long, exciting tale is compressed into only a few stanzas, full of action.

In the ballad, "Sir Patrick Spens," the minstrel sang a typical tale of **treachery**, heroism, and tragedy. The story was probably based on a true incident. It has the "do-or-die" feeling of the time in which it took place.

Many of the words in the ballad have old Scottish spelling. Most of the words can be guessed at from the context. A few are numbered with the modern spelling or meaning at the bottom of the page.

Sir Patrick Spens

by Unknown Author

The king sits in Dunfermling town
Sits on his throne so fine,
"O where will I get a gude skipper
To sail this ship o' mine?"

O up and spake an eldern knight,
Sat at the king's right knee:
"Sir Patrick Spens is the best sailor
That ever sail'd the sea."

Our king has written a letter,
And seal'd it with his hand,
And sent it to Sir Patrick Spens,
Was walking on the strand.

"To Noroway, to Noroway,
To Noroway o'ver the faem[1];
The king's daughter o' Noroway,
'Tis thou must bring her hame."

The first word that Sir Patrick read,
A loud laugh laughed he;
The next word that Sir Patrick read,
The tear blinded his e'e.

"O who is this has done this deed
This ill deed unto me,
To send us out, at this time o' year,
To sail upon the sea?

[1]Foam

"Be it wind, be it weet, be it hail, be it sleet,
Our ship must sail the faem;
The king's daughter o' Noroway,
'Tis we must fetch her hame.

"Make haste, make haste, my merry men all;
Our gude ship sails the morn."–
"Now ever alack, my master dear,
I fear a deadly storm.

"Late, late yestreen[2] I saw the new moone
Wi' the auld moone in her arm;
And I fear, I fear, my master dear,
That we will come to harm."

They hadna sail'd a league, a league,
A league but barely three,
When the sky grew dark, and the wind blew loud,
And angry grew the sea.

The anchors broke, the topmast split,
It was sic[3] a deadly storm:
And the waves came owre the broken ship
Till a' her sides were torn.

O loath, loath, were our gude Scots lords
To wet their cork-heel'd shoon;
But lang or a' the play was play'd
Their hats they swam aboon.[4]

O lang, lang may the ladies sit,
Wi' their fans into their hand,
Before they see Sir Patrick Spens
Come sailing to the strand.

And lang, lang may the maidens sit
Wi' their gold kames in their hair.
A-waiting for their ain dear loves,
For them they'll see nae mair.

Half-owre, half-owre to Aberdour,
'Tis fifty fathoms deep;
And there lies gude Sir Patrick Spens,
Wi' the Scots lords at his feet.

[2]yesterevening
[3]such
[4]above their heads

What are some of the major characteristics of a ballad that can be seen in "Sir Patrick Spens?"

4.1 _____

_____

_____

_____

_____

Use your dictionary to look up the complete meanings of the following vocabulary words.

4.2 minstrel _____

_____

4.3 dialogue _____

_____

4.4 ballad _____

_____

4.5 compress _____

_____

4.6 treachery _____

_____

4.7 rely _____

_____

4.8 limerick _____

_____

Complete the following words studies.

4.9 Write the five vocabulary words in the last activity that have the accent or stress on the first syllable.

a. _____ b. _____ c. _____

d. _____ e. _____

4.10 Write the vocabulary word that is not spelled with an *i* but has the long /*i*/ sound.

_____

4.11 Write the two vocabulary words that have three syllables

a. _____ b. _____

Lullabies. A lullaby is a form of ballad which is usually sung to children to hush them to sleep. Most lullabies are short and have gentle or restful words. "Rock-a-Bye Baby" is a typical lullaby.

 Complete this activity.

4.12 Look up any music books (get your parent or your music teacher to help you) and select a lullaby.

a. Book title: _____

b. Author: _____

c. Publisher: _____

d. Title of lullaby: _____

e. The text (words) of the song: _____

_____

_____

_____

_____

_____

_____

_____

_____

_____

_____

_____

_____

_____

_____

_____

TEACHER CHECK _____ _____

initials   date

Add the correct suffixes to the following base words so that the words fit the definition.
Use these suffixes: *-ive, -y, -ible, -ish, -less, -al,* and *-ic.*

4.13 fault _____   imperfect

4.14 attract _____   pleasing

4.15 music _____   melodious

4.16 cheer _____   gloomy

4.17 flex _____   can be bent

4.18 instruct _____   educational

4.19 room _____   lots of room

4.20 artist _____   creative and pleasing

4.21 clown _____   act like a clown

4.22 weight _____   heavy

4.23 secret _____   to keep quiet about something

4.24 rest _____   not to be able to sit still

Form new words by adding the suffix *-er* and *-est* to the following words. Remember, if a word ends in *y,* you change the *y* to *i* when you add a suffix. If a word ends with a consonant, sometimes you double the consonant before adding the suffix.

An example is given.

big	**bigger**	**biggest**
4.25 wet	_____	_____
4.26 thin	_____	_____
4.27 merry	_____	_____
4.28 happy	_____	_____
4.29 silly	_____	_____
4.30 red	_____	_____
4.31 jolly	_____	_____
4.32 bold	_____	_____
4.33 near	_____	_____
4.34 thirsty	_____	_____

WORD PLAY

Riddles and **limericks** both play on words. Limericks have a rhyming pattern like most poems, whereas a riddle does not have any particular pattern. A riddle can be put to verse, although it is usually stated in a question form. A limerick is meant to be clever or funny, whereas a riddle is just clever.

Riddles. A riddle is a trick question sometimes put in the form of a poem. In the Middle Ages telling riddles was quite an art. In many **mythologies** answering a riddle was often used as a test. In Greek mythology the Sphinx (a terrible creature, part-woman, part-lion, part-bird) would **waylay** travelers and ask them a riddle. If they could not answer it, she would kill them.

The riddle the Sphinx is supposed to have asked is "What goes on four legs in the morning, on two legs at noon, and on three legs at night?"

Could you have solved this riddle? The answer is "Man, who goes on 'all fours' as a baby, walks on two legs from the time he is a child until he is old, and then uses a cane to help his aging legs."

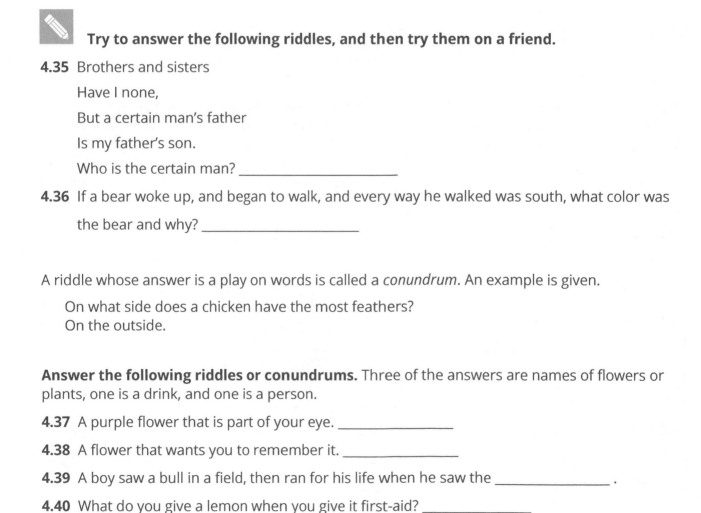

Try to answer the following riddles, and then try them on a friend.

4.35 Brothers and sisters

Have I none,

But a certain man's father

Is my father's son.

Who is the certain man? _____

4.36 If a bear woke up, and began to walk, and every way he walked was south, what color was

the bear and why? _____

A riddle whose answer is a play on words is called a *conundrum*. An example is given.

On what side does a chicken have the most feathers?
On the outside.

Answer the following riddles or conundrums. Three of the answers are names of flowers or plants, one is a drink, and one is a person.

4.37 A purple flower that is part of your eye. _____

4.38 A flower that wants you to remember it. _____

4.39 A boy saw a bull in a field, then ran for his life when he saw the _____ .

4.40 What do you give a lemon when you give it first-aid? _____

4.41 A name for an ant who lives in a house? an _____

Find the hidden words in the following words. You are given a clue to each hidden word.

An example is given.

Word	Clue to Hidden Word	Hidden Word
loaf	a clumsy person	oaf

4.42 glance   A knight carries one   _____

4.43 coop   the sound a dove makes   _____

4.44 dinner   a very loud noise   _____

4.45 globe   a part of your ear   _____

4.46 decanter   a kind of gallop   _____

4.47 kayak   A kind of long-haired ox   _____

4.48 facsimile   a figure of speech talked about in this LIFEPAC   _____

4.49 abduct   a part of your eye   _____

Limericks. A limerick is a short poem that follows a particular pattern. It is usually funny and clever. Edward Lear, an English poet, made limericks very popular.

Here are two limericks written by Florence Priest. Read them aloud so that you can get the feel of the rhythm. Rhythm plays a major role when constructing limericks. As you read the limericks aloud, beat the rhythm with your hand.

Hint:
In the first limerick, read *Wyo.* as the full name of the state, and make *glo.* and *ro.* rhyme with it.

A couple who lived in Wyo.
Used to walk hand in hand in the glo.
    Once during a tiff,
    They walked off a cliff,
Which proves you should watch where you're ro.

by Florence Priest

A lady who lived on the Verde
Considered herself very perde,
    'Til once in a mirror
    She saw herself clirror
As not only ugly but derde.

by Florence Priest

Answer these questions. Notice the play on words the poet has used in these two limericks.

4.50 What do the invented words, *perde* and *derde* stand for?

a. _____   b. _____

4.51 What does *clirror* really stand for? _____

4.52 Why did the poet change the spelling of these three words?

_____

_____

4.53 What do the abbreviations *Wyo., glo.,* and *ro.* stand for?

a. _____   b. _____   c. _____

Notice that in limericks, lines one, two, and five all rhyme with each other and consist of three beats to a line. Lines three and four also rhyme with each other and are much shorter, having only two beats to a line. Discuss the rhythm with your teacher first, and read many limericks aloud, before attempting to write a limerick yourself.

Write two limericks of your own. Share them with a friend.

4.54 There was a _____ from _____

Who _____

_____

_____

_____

4.55 There was a _____ from _____

Who _____

_____

_____

_____

TEACHER CHECK _____ _____

initials   date

4.56 Make a small book containing all the poems you have written for this LIFEPAC (make sure you have worked to improve each one). Have your teacher select a corner of the room for a book display.

TEACHER CHECK _____ _____
initials   date

Complete the crossword puzzle.

4.57 The clues are on the following page.

Across

3. The repetition of letters in a sentence is called _____

6. A vocabulary word given in this LIFEPAC meaning to *cross over*

7. Means *the opposite of*

8. A word meaning *bright*

10. Another word meaning *boring*

11. A sort of dictionary that puts words into categories

12. A vocabulary word given in this LIFEPAC meaning *in a sleepy way*

14. A vocabulary word in this LIFEPAC that means *easy to bend*

15. When a word or term is overused, it becomes a _____

16. Another term for *verse*

Down

1. A funny type of poem that has five lines (with the first, second, and fifth lines rhyming with each other)

2. The surname of a poet who made limericks very popular

3. The name of a type of contraction which is formed from the first letters or syllable of a compound term, phrase, or title

4. When you add syllables, letters, suffixes, or any type of endings to a word, these are called _____ endings

5. The name for a riddle that is a play on words

9. Figures of speech that call one thing something else

13. The last name of a popular modern author of children's books who invents lots of new words

15. The last name of the author of *The Canterbury Tales.*

Palindromes. In this LIFEPAC you have been made aware that playing with words helps enrich our language. We invent words, put words together to form compound words, abbreviate phrases to form acronyms, find hidden words, and rhyme words.

A curious thing has been noticed about certain words. They can be read backwards or forwards without changing the word or its meaning. Such words are called palindromes. Two examples of single word *palindromes* are *sees* and *rotor*.

An example of a longer palindrome is

"Madam, I'm Adam."

What are the following palindromes? Remember, the letters in a palindrome can be read either way without changing the spelling of the word.

An example is given.

another name for a seed in a fruit ___pip___

4.58 a baby wears this when it eats _____

4.59 a boy's name _____

4.60 to peek or look inside something _____

4.61 you can see with it _____

4.62 a short form for father _____

4.63 a short word for a flower that you give on Mother's Day _____

4.64 a female sheep _____

4.65 an Inuit boat _____

4.66 a slang word for a joke _____

4.67 the name of a famous woman in the Old Testament _____

4.68 another word for midday _____

Make a list of palindromes that you come across.

4.69 See if you can trick your parents or friends by thinking of palindromes that they cannot answer. Ask your teacher if you could help set up a class competition for palindrome collecting.

TEACHER CHECK _____ _____
                        initials   date

SPELLING AND HANDWRITING

The spelling words are all homonyms. The handwriting practice will be of the capital letters *M*, *N*, and *W*.

Spelling. Learn the words in Spelling Words-4. These words are all homonyms. Put your imagination to work to make memory aids to help you remember them.

Learn to spell the words from Spelling Words-4.

SPELLING WORDS-4

gamble	sole	waive
gambol	soul	wave
cannon	clime	sear
canon	climb	seer

Copy the spelling words in your best handwriting, placing them in alphabetical order.

4.70 a. _____ b. _____ c. _____

d. _____ e. _____ f. _____

g. _____ h. _____ i. _____

j. _____ k. _____ l. _____

Use your dictionary and find the meanings of the following words.

4.71 gambol _____

4.72 clime _____

4.73 seer _____

4.74 sear _____

4.75 waive _____

4.76 sole _____

4.77 cannon _____

Unscramble these words. They all can be found in your Spelling Words-4 list.

4.78 a. eres   _____   b. iewva   _____

    c. leos   _____   d. blimc   _____

    e. milec   _____   f. bamgel   _____

    g. raes   _____   h. noncan   _____

Handwriting. Capital *M* and *N* are almost identical. Keep the sides of the letters straight and fairly narrow. All three letters, *M*, *N*, and *W* have curls at the beginning of the downward stroke.

Copy each of the following words.

Note: Because they are names of cities, they begin with a capital letter.

4.79

Milwaukee   New York
Washington

ABC   **Ask your teacher to give you a practice spelling test of Spelling Words-4.** Restudy the words you missed.

Before you take this last Self Test, you may want to do one or more of these self checks.

1. _____ Read the objectives. See if you can do them.
2. _____ Restudy the material related to any objectives that you cannot do.
3. _____ Use the **SQ3R** study procedure to review the material:
   a. **S**can the sections.
   b. **Q**uestion yourself.
   c. **R**ead to answer your questions.
   d. **R**ecite the answers to yourself.
   e. **R**eview areas you did not understand.
4. _____ Review all vocabulary, activities, and Self Tests, writing a correct answer for every wrong answer.

SELF TEST 4

Match these items (each answer, 2 points).

4.01 _____ these men sang for their supper

4.02 _____ these were given as a test in ancient mythologies

4.03 _____ a story put to song

4.04 _____ a man who obeyed his king when he knew he would probably die

4.05 _____ a song that makes a child drowsy

4.06 _____ he wrote limericks

4.07 _____ a riddle that is a play on words

4.08 _____ words that can be spelled in reverse without altering

4.09 _____ author of "Sir Patrick Spens"

a. Sir Patrick Spens

b. Edward Lear

c. palindromes

d. conundrum

e. minstrels

f. sphinx

g. unknown

h. riddles

i. lullaby

j. ballad

What are four main characteristics of a ballad (each answer, 3 points)?

4.010 _____

4.011 _____

4.012 _____

4.013 _____

Write the correct pair of homonyms in the blanks. Select the words from the list (each sentence, 3 points).

mien	clime	liar	mean
climb	lyre	peal	lone
soul	canon	rein	horde
seer	reign	hoard	sear
cannon	loan	sole	peel

4.014 The a. _____ survivor did not want to ask for a b. _____ from the bank.

4.015 The thieves hid their stolen a. _____ from the b. _____ of policemen.

4.016 She gave a a. _____ of laughter when she had to b. _____ the potatoes.

4.017 It is easier to a. _____ in a sunny b. _____ than a snowy one.

4.018 The poor old a. _____ kept complaining about the b. _____ of her feet.

4.019 The a. _____ old hermit had an ugly b. _____ .

4.020 You are a a. _____ if you say I stole your b. _____ .

4.021 It is against the a. _____ of the church to blow a town up with a b. _____ .

4.022 The a. _____ ing queen had a golden b. _____ for her horse.

4.023 The a. _____ was not wise enough to prevent being b. _____ ed by the fire.

Match these items (each answer, 2 points).

4.024 _____ Ezra Pound

4.025 _____ cinquain

4.026 _____ Lewis Carroll

4.027 _____ acronyms

4.028 _____ topsy-turvy

4.029 _____ sift

4.030 _____ tenacious

a. wrote a famous book about a white rabbit and a little girl

b. to refuse to give up

c. an American poet

d. to separate particles

e. five-line poem

f. tricky and dangerous

g. formed from first letter of each word in a title

h. in great disorder

Answer true or false (each answer, 1 point).

4.031 _____ My fingers and toes are attached to my limbs.

4.032 _____ A narrative poem is very short and has a funny shape.

4.033 _____ Free verse is not bound by any rules.

4.034 _____ A poet must economize with words.

4.035 _____ Blades of grass, leaves, and flower petals are not pliant.

4.036 _____ A monotonous voice is exciting to listen to.

4.037 _____ When the years fly by, they are fleeting.

4.038 _____ A wooden expression is a happy one.

4.039 _____ Similes and metaphors are figures of speech.

4.040 _____ Alliteration is another word for rhythm.

4.041 _____ Rhythm and rhyme mean the same thing.

Name five types of poetic forms you have studied and written in this LIFEPAC (3 points each).

4.042 _____

4.043 _____

4.044 _____

4.045 _____

4.046 _____

80 / 100   **SCORE** _____   **TEACHER** _____ _____
                                                    initials   date

ABC   **Take your spelling test of Spelling Words-4.**

↺   **Before taking the LIFEPAC Test, you may want to do one or more of these self checks.**

1. _____ Read the objectives. See if you can do them.

2. _____ Restudy the material related to any objectives that you cannot do.

3. _____ Use the **SQ3R** study procedure to review the material.

4. _____ Review activities, Self Tests, and LIFEPAC vocabulary words.

5. _____ Restudy areas of weakness indicated by the last Self Test.

6. _____ Review all Spelling Words in this LIFEPAC.